Claire Caldwell

GOLD
RUSH

Claire Caldwell

GOLD RUSH

Invisible Publishing

Halifax & Prince Edward County

Library and Archives Canada Cataloguing in Publication

Title: Gold rush / Claire Caldwell.

Names: Caldwell, Claire, 1988- author.

Description: Poems.

Identifiers:
Canadiana (print) 20190155906
Canadiana (ebook) 20200165739
ISBN 9781988784465 (softcover)
ISBN 9781988784496 (HTML)

Classification: LCC PS8605.A45685 G65 2020 | DDC C811/.6—dc23

Edited by Leigh Nash
Cover and interior design by Megan Fildes
With thanks to type designer Rod McDonald

Invisible Publishing is committed to protecting our natural environment. As part of our efforts, both the cover and interior of this book are printed on acid-free 100% post-consumer recycled fibres.

Printed and bound in Canada

Invisible Publishing | Halifax & Prince Edward County
www.invisiblepublishing.com

We acknowledge for their financial support of our publishing program the Canada Council for the Arts, the Ontario Arts Council, and the Government of Canada.

For Stephen, my partner in the wilderness.
And for Moira, who is always up for an adventure.

PART ONE: Frontier Diaries

PART TWO: Backcountry Almanac

PART THREE: After the Gold Rush

PART ONE

Frontier Diaries

Shifter

It starts with the mammoth shin
in your parents' garage, holed up in a lean-to
of cross-country skis. Then it's the maybe-owl,
ptarmigrouse, mating call mistaken
for motorboat. Nothing
is what it used to be: the Gerber jar on the piano
filled not with spare buttons but prehistoric
horse teeth. You wobble
into bed on four woolly ankles.
Wake in the greenhouse, fists swollen
with chard. No one warned you
your body could feel like coming home
knowing strangers have been there.
Empty frame on the dresser,
bent fork in your underwear
drawer. But now you recognize a carnivore
slope in women's shoulders, whiskers
stubbling their jaws.
Stop asking what will come
loping toward you, start with "When?"
Your hair splits: an oil spill
around your horns.

Actresses Fording Dyea River
on the Chilkoot Trail, 1897
After the photo by Frank La Roche

Applause had softened us. What could we glean
from the aspens' sarcastic ovations, the ravens
tossing lozenge tins and nails where we expected

bouquets? We curtsied through July's long
curtain call, thighs rolling beneath our skirts
like otters, satchels pregnant with silk

and lard. We memorized lines of pine tar,
crushed mosquitoes. The wolves in the wings did not
return our keening. Our stockings dried

after midnight: a brief intermission
of ankles, bleached coronets of caribou antlers.
No one lowered the house lights.

In the third act, the wolf pack
poured past us like a set of rapids.
We drove our fists into their current.
Never sank to our knees.

Frontier Diaries

Erasure poems based on the personal accounts
of homesteading women, 1867–2016

Labour

I will always be here.
I gave birth to a home.
My choices are lumps
in my throat:
second daughter,
sleep, start pushing.
A gap in attention.
Beans for years.
Ascent

Ascent

The mountain advanced.
I shed my corset.
Soon, I was panting.
On, on, on, on.
Don't look down.
Throbbing, hungry,
fire in deep snow.

Winter

I was flannel-lined
fur-trimmed
and chattering.
Sparrows hung
above the mess hall.
Seven women
promptly moved
to Toronto
for recalibration.
An emergency
contingent of huskies
seemed to sing
of white gasoline.

Growth

The idea of building a husband
broke in February. By October,
he was warm. For comparison,
our neighbour is growing children,
and we hope to begin work
on a solar system. For now,
our tiny home is full.

Theft

One day, I vanished.
Was it Camp Robber?
The child, the baby's
closest friend?
Wolf or grandfather?
Long-haired willow,
canine teeth
behind our cabin.
Impossible:
I could not venture
outside the house.

Shelter

Cold will eclipse us.
This morning, ice
and no possibility
of being warm. The season
was faded and sparkling,
a long meditation on the past.
We assembled in the kitchen.
Heaping lake fog skirted the house
and the woods reached,
I think, to England.

Fever

First nurses, then the silence
of mines. 11:00, 10:00,
2:30? Buckskin pulled
over skull. Black fire.
A moccasined eagle grins
and asks me—

Faith

This season
is a white church,
and my hair
will get in all the crevices.
I resign myself
to a pale adventure.
Real housewives
remember every reason
to be alive.

Father

God of mischief.
God waiting upstairs.

Bucking, shaking,
quivering God.

God of ladies
who never prepare.

God is a total mess.
He wants cheese
and wool and pies.

Every woman
creates God
with her hands.

Luxuries

Sometimes the grouse
were shooting stars.
Sometimes drowsy.
The lake a guitar,
rain a tall evergreen
or a fur robe.
I contain a canyon
of roaring horses
and a small tent
for rest.

Commitment

Bread is both
inconvenience
and rapture.
I increase and
increase
the provisions.
I married a land
where bread is a lover:
the taste of sacrifice
and shame. Dread rose,
became energy.
My fist turned the world
upon the world.

Homestead Rescue

Give me your cracked
foundations, your chainsaw
accidents, your decapitated
hens. Give me carbon monoxide
poisoning, water tank
contaminated by a family
of leering possums.

I'm the patron saint of failing
homesteads, and I've come
with my camera crew.
I've brought my son, a felled larch
hewn into muscle.
My daughter, cut
from a lynx's womb.

She'll rip apart your sibling
rivalry to make space
for a meat smoker. He'll strip
the tree limbs throwing tantrums
on your roof. Firewood or fourth
wall for your outhouse?
We'll prep you to survive

the winter—but only
if you shriek
before commercial breaks.
You own everything
between bedrock and sharp-shinned
hawk and you're still hungry?
That's embarrassing.

Show me your palest offspring.
I'll fill him with buckshot
lust, force him to field dress
a doe. The more he cries, the higher
the ratings, but don't worry—I'll
pull the trigger. This is TV.
We need to kill something.

The Hillary Step Is Gone

Everest just ain't the same.
In the good old days, we fashioned crampons
from the jaws of nurse sharks, imported elephant
spines to lay across crevasses.

We huffed through beluga lungs
until they puckered like used condoms,
then sent them jellyfishing off to China.

Wind was an older brother—
his knee on your neck, head
in the toilet: *flusssssshhhh*.

But we weren't pussies.
Grew chest hair thick enough to weave
into thermals, roasted pack mules
at Base Camp, cured leftover
intestines for rope.

The math is one death
per hundred feet, but the summit's
been going downhill for decades.
Now all a guy has to do is fall

asleep. Our reputations scarred by GORE-TEX
mummies, oxygen canisters that'll last
long enough for archaeologists
to assume we were deep-sea divers.

But we earned this: the right to stand
on the earth's most flamboyant cowlick,
poke selfie sticks in its scalp like pins.

What's the point of a mountain
if we can't climb it? Who else
can we blame if we don't make it down?

Transmission from Jupiter
For the Juno spacecraft

I expected Europa's beaches
to have surf shacks, coconuts
frothing with lunar slush. Callisto's ice
machine clacks like an asteroid belt

of dentures. If one of these moons
has a breakfast buffet, it's occluded
by dust. Has the Red Spot
gotten smaller, or have I

just grown up? Days are short here,
and when it rains, the sky is a dive bar
strung with Christmas light. Still, it's nice
to get away from life. Haven't worried

about zebra mussels since Mars.
Siberian tigers, well, that's harder.
There's muscle under this planet's
marmalade, and I've got a hand

on her flank. We're going for a prowl
around the campfire. The forest is starry,
eyed. Keep your head in the flames
and you'll miss us. You'll miss us anyway.

PART TWO

Backcountry Almanac

Canoe Lake

For Tom Thomson

Water goosed by palette knife,
rocks with a few more years
licked off. I'm sure you get this
a lot—girls who stretched like birches
around your grave, each summer
a smudge of pine and sapphire,
grapefruit sky. A canoe
in every frame. Ten Augusts
for me to see this place
wasn't blank before you,
that time is more paddle
than paintbrush. Your ghost
the only one we knew
how to look for—
that shimmer of linseed oil
at twilight swelling into boat
and body, loon
gliding right on through.

Backcountry Almanac

Our guide is a goddess
in quick-dry shorts,
braid that could save you
from drowning. Says
weather's just a function
of how many swims
you take. A leech
in the pannikin
is worth her laughter.
The value of blisters
is praise. We slough
sunscreen, export
freckles, import spit
and bug spray.
The portage ends
when we hit the lake,
but meanwhile,
she's mythic: Boreal
centaur, all hull
and hiking boots,
mud-spattered legs.
Guardian of time
and trail mix; nineteen
but seems immortal.
And yes, she says,
if a girl falls
in a forest
she leaves a trace.

Girls Gone Wild
After Ariel Gordon

Paddling done for the day, we strip
to our hiking boots and pitch ourselves

like cold cereal

into water with a black-spruce
complexion. Our pale bums breach

egg- to heart-shaped

as we unsnarl our teenage muscles,
shake out the J-strokes, the kilometres

sharply lobed or toothed

Grummans perched like eagles
on our shoulder blades. Nine girls

resinous and glandular

air-dry on Precambrian shield.
We don't see ourselves

long-burning, sweet-smelling

or we see excessively.
I sneak glimpses

inconspicuous, small

of stomachs flat as wannigans, portage-
thickened thighs. F. grabs my hand

likely a mistake

and leads me to blueberries.
Her collarbone gleams

long, thin, linear

like a cedar thwart. I chew the fruit,
ignore the seeds

with creeping roots

that burrow inside me.
F. hasn't shaved

wiry, barbed awns

since she lasered her armpit hair
in Grade Eight. I want to stop growing

pear-shaped, fleshy hips

and this makes me ashamed.
At fifteen, I don't yet know the difference

important wild

between being watched and being seen.
Between the want to touch, the want to be.

Cusp

Seven summers here, but I've never seen stars
like this. He chews a Fuzzy Peach to chase

a cigarette. Sunrise tastes like corn syrup
and nicotine. He gives me hieroglyphs

Sharpied to a scrap of birch bark,
Arts and Crafts roses, pink eye. I swallow

the Milky Way. Flicker and froth,
then ditch him on the canoe docks.

Strip, dive, kick: my comet tail hissing, held
in the lake's wet orbit. Oh, yes, this. This. This

celestial body. These ten fingertips. Only I
can trace the lines that stitch my limbs together.

I rise like the Big Dipper.
Wear the moon like a breast.

Occasional Poem

Sometimes a person
just has to drive
to the lake.
Undress.

Sometimes the day
is a dead trout
and night slams over it
like a cooler's lid.

Sometimes she hits
send, snaps
her wrist. The reply
a flare or a tiny Viking

funeral followed
by a splash.
She is silent
as a screen.

Fills her bottom lip
with frog eggs.
Microbeads.

Sometimes the reeds
feel like hair.
Sometimes it's her hair.
Someone else's fist.

Grizzly Lake Trail

There are risks
we failed to calculate: rust-fungused

rose hips, mineral-deficient ground squirrels
craving shoelaces. Twenty-year-olds

trail us in Chuck Taylors, stretched sweaters,
JanSports sloshing with cans of PBR.

We're not moms, but we *were*
camp counsellors. We worry

about wicking layers, supportive
boots. The valley bloats with invisible

grizzlies, a boulder field of broken ankles.
Vegan hot dogs sweat in our bear-

proof canister for a dozen klicks.
We pass a single dad from Coquitlam

who thinks the sun shines out
his dromedary bag. He shares unsolicited

waterfall pics, brags about his preteens
while they negotiate the talus, how they

don't carry extra weight.
At the communal campsite, a fever

unzips my sleeping bag. I try not to
throw up in the protected ecozone, don't

make it. Two older women who've been hiking
together since we learned to walk

gift me a Thermos of broth, a sleeve
of electrolytes. The JanSport girls sweetly

offer toothpaste, pot. Three Advil get me back
to the trailhead where the car won't start.

Sounds a Raven Makes

Smoker's laugh, bedsprings, stone skipped

across the river. Raven imitated by kids

flapping parka sleeves on a skating rink.

Raven imitated by a miner who's not seen

people in days. Rusty bike chain,

3:00 a.m. phone call, snow melting off roof.

Raven imitated by raven. Coin dropped

in a tip jar. Dog locked in a truck.

Sounds a River Makes

Gas leak, ventilator, bear clicking its teeth.

Twelve hundred caribou hooves on frost.

Lips around bottle, bottle slurring

on bar. Rattling aspen, dusky grouse,

sheets drying outside. Grandmothers

stuffing envelopes in a high school gym.

Sex in a sleeping bag, house on fire.

A children's choir after one kid

faints, before the rest start to sing.

Sounds the Snow Makes

Knife spreading peanut butter, first bite

of toast. Scalp massage in a beanbag chair.

Woof of blood against eardrums, crumbs

between sheets. Wool socks nipped by concrete.

Sweatpants pooled on the floor.

Toddler fists pounding a futon,

the toddler's half-hour nap. Swish

of eyelashes. Spider rocked

by breath.

How to See a Moose

I

Pack three clementines and an emergency
turkey drumstick, even if you don't
eat meat. Forget matches.

Ski until your hamstrings droop
like the waistband of your long johns,
family heirlooms circa 1992.

As your sweat caramelizes, the sky
will swell like a pan of milk
on a low flame.

Trespass at the shuttered summer camp
where God appeared

as a thirteen-year-old girl in a Laser II dinghy,
the Authority on physical flaws.
She called you Chicken Legs,

so you tipped
the sailboat (let She who is without sin
lift the first butt cheek).

The breeze
a convenient scapegoat,
a more convincing deity.

II

Pass the guide shack, the mummified
kayaks, the snow-dipped fire pit where white
nineteen-year-olds shook buckskin

rumps and feather headdresses
twice a summer. You
were the white child

who never questioned this
until the one summer it was edgy
to complain. Even that year

you wore red. Waved ferns.
Approached the flames.

III

Remember when you got your period
in the wet grass above the riding ring.

Forced to watch the horse kids
coax Sky and Shadow and Parsley into winning
ribbons. No one else was allowed
to move or speak for fear

of trampling. Three swampy hours,
certain your ass was a crime scene.

IV

Think: something so big should be
self-evident. Chocolate stain on white T-shirt.
Chatter of saplings high-fiving antlers.
Bare branches snapped off flanks.

Eight hundred pounds of potential
violence, mute as the rifle
in the cottage crawlspace.

Except the moose ghosts on ahead of you.
Uncontained.

V

Take nothing.

You already have
the green cabins,
cedar-ribbed canoes,
dining hall with its rafters

and plaques
commemorating teens
who went into the woods
and came out
hairier,

white diving tower,
legend of the kid who hit bottom
neck-first. Banana Boat
haze of the swim docks,
sun-faded PFDs—

You own none of it.
That's the point.

VI

Consider the alternatives:

Trophy mounted above a walnut
bar, tinsel and tambourine
cuffing each antler.

Plastic model muzzled by a surgeon's
mask, ill-fitting scrubs, shill for the dental
practice beside the cemetery.

Lice-ridden museum specimen,
snout stuck inches from papier mâché grass.

Snake of Muskoka-bound SUVs scaled
with ruby brake lights. Slither interrupted
by tumour of bone and hide.

VII

Cross the border
between dock and ice.
Stake a ski pole
where you used to knife

to the bottom, scan rocks
and algae for three
breaststrokes, rise—

panicked hooves
in your chest.

Always a drill,
but you were still
afraid of what
you'd find down there.

Look at it.

The ungulate shape
of this land,
stolen

so you could pretend
to rescue an imaginary
child from drowning.

VIII

Yes, those
are moose tracks.
Nail holes or
knuckles
in drywall.
Something was here.
Now it's missing.

PART THREE

After the Gold Rush

Canadian Ninja Warrior

The first season will feature a snowmobile,
melting sea ice, and a narwhal's tusk.
One bounce on the permafrost
trampoline to grab a goose leg.
Swing yourself to the tip of the V.

How's your grip strength? We'll reinstate
the salmon ladder when we can make it
sustainable. For now, it's a knuckle hop
across the tar sands on a raft
of Hudson's Bay blankets.

Next season, try Niagara Falls in a lobster trap.
Outswim a coyote through the Red River
Floodway. Contestants who can't name
the traditional territory they squat on
won't get their Tim's at the finish line.

Please note: making love in a canoe
is no longer considered extreme.
Our sponsors are not responsible
for the boil water advisory;
you should try their ice wine.

After the Gold Rush

The dry century retreated, left mustangs
bucking across brothel walls. The sky coughed
up its molars. Mushrooms bruised every lawn.

Spruce got wasted on spongy permafrost
while cabins kissed sloppily. Jaws and antlers
surged through sprays of reindeer

moss like breaching whales.
Night returned earlier than expected,
hitched a ride from Whitehorse with a cloud

who'd chugged the Bering Sea.
Beavers redeveloped tailing ponds
with moats of squirrel grass, raspberries.

We bleached the forest
with headlamps, sautéed milk caps,
lashed chives to our backs like arrows.

Sometimes rain was just weather, the flare
of fangs in the willows an injured
dog. The ice bridge atrophied to a catwalk.

The only snow a defiant strain of strep throat.

The Hedgehog Officer Reflects on Her Tenure

There was no hedgehog roadshow
that first spring. For weeks
the job was a bleak affair of nets
and tags and freezers.

Who could blame me for sleeping
with the fox commissioner?
I was starved for success,
eager to waddle up the food chain.

Besides, I couldn't resist
those ankles. Fang-sharp,
freckled, fur soft as an ear.

Couldn't the locals trim their own
blackthorn, drill tasteful holes
in their gates? Yes, bramble strangled

the live-cam wires and the lone
hedgehog hotspot was a furrow
in my duvet. But I *did* work.

Over dill and pheasant eggs,
the commissioner and I railed
against the Department
for Badger Advancement.

When the gossips from the Snail Society
came sneaking around my compost pile,
I chased them off with lavender
spray. I daresay, my legacy

will be that the Orwell flooded
only once in my three-year stint.
But my greatest act of conservation

was teaching him to bite
without splitting my skin.
Exquisite, to be reminded
I was meat.

Saturday Animals
After Don Summerhayes

You make me wild,
a choice between love
and nesting with the bats.
I resist peanut butter
toast and decaf lingerie.
I have to jog before asparagus
on the pillow. Let the turtles
out: their darling seals
nose up to the window.

Dear Space Boyfriend

You're lagging. In the absence
of video chat, I've posted thirst traps
across the Great Lakes, typed DMs
into Superior's waves. BTW, I've heard

the Canadarm can personalize
any river, curl it like a silver chain.
For my birthday, I'd like the Saint Lawrence
to spell my name. Space Boyfriend,

there's an ozone between us, but I'm
more tethered than ever. Last week in
Alaska, a black bear crashed through
a skylight into a pile of cupcakes.

I know how hard you've worked
to be weightless. It's just—
shouldn't microgravity make your heart
pump harder?

I've turned on read receipts, two bright
checks above our starless city.
Use them to navigate. I want you to kneel
on the atmosphere's glass floor until it breaks.

Which Endangered Species Are You?
Take Our Quiz!

Select a habitat: montane cloud forest,
cleared ski run, artificial chimpanzee
colony, Turkey Creek. Are you susceptible

to white band disease? If you said
"chytridiomycosis," you might not live
to see the last pine plucked

from the Sierra de Juárez. If *Acacia Veronica*
ends things, how long will it take you to die
of heartbreak? Are you the smallest

and rarest of your kind? Mount Sinai's
gold crown: are you whorled? Describe
(in five words or fewer) the taste of flying

lemur. How many deer does it take
to pulp a sapling? On a map,
colour the places you've grazed since 2008.

(This quiz does not accept responsibility
for any misuse of this information.)
Was a predatory snail introduced?

Was your sister electrocuted?
Were your brother's bones crushed

into capsules? Rank your satisfaction
with the Lichen Specialist Group.
On a scale of least concern to
critical, tell us how you heard

about this quiz. Our algorithm predicts
over 28,000 possible extinctions.
Analytics suggest your results will hinge

on followers and forestry
effluents. If you've been spotted
since the nineties, please click here.

Last Night on Earth
For the Bramble Cay Melomys

First moon in claw time,
second moon swinging
from the silver tree.
Ocean a tail's length
closer. Cheeks
full of purslane,
no pink pups to feed.

Where has the sand gone?
Shark bones croon
to their brothers.
Loggerheads circle,
strips of land
in their teeth.

Black rocks, be like clouds
and blow here. Coral,
become bridge. Petrels, light
on this russet spine
and lift—

For the Toronto Zoo Elephants

We never expected them to leave.
No matter how often our talent bolted
for California, we took it personally.

Wasn't the moon the elephant's footprint?
Didn't we give their babies names?

We married beneath arches carved
to imitate the Stonehenge of their bellies.
Groomed ski hills till they were firm
as ivory, taught novices to tuck poles
up like tusks.

We didn't visit much in winter,
except when the crochet league broke into
their enclosure, rolling chunky
wool over trunks like purled prophylactics.

The public radio station broadcast their first day
at the sanctuary. Our windshields buzzed
with trumpeting. How could they
sound so joyful

when it was *our* sky
that matched their skin?
Snow penned us in.

Three elephants' worth of wet
confetti, from Scarborough to Kipling.

Rubbernecking

We surround the koi pond
like paparazzi. The frog vaults,
impatient with the reverse camera flashes
of our shadows. We've got all day, but he stays
disguised in dead bamboo and algae
aviators, so we swoop down
to the river for a blind item
on a certain swan with a kinky leg.

The pedestrian bridge offers primetime
viewing for mallardultery: ducklings
hatched upstream of their daddies.
At magic hour, a private security firm
manned by Canada geese
hisses us back into our SUVs.

No sweat; we've got a tip on a beaver
who tried to cross the highway,
purr up in time for her perp walk.

A spokesperson tweets about woodchuck
quotas, sustainable logging, and later
deletes it. Before we can retract
even a single pixel, the frog scoops us
with a throatful of rumours
then rockets into the dusk
of a blue heron's esophagus.

The Wilderness Online

While the TSA trains birds to attack drones
in protected air space, a sales associate
at a suburban Nissan dealership feeds quinoa
to eastern cottontails—hot lunch for the falcons
nine-to-fiving it at air traffic control.

Three test drives later, the associate embarks
on the *Eat, Pray, Love* of underwear shopping.
It's raining vaccine-laced M&M's
in the mall parking lot, which approximates

a prairie. Where's the dating app
full of park rangers with helicopter access
and glorified Nerf guns? She's supposed to root
for the black-footed ferret, not the flea-borne
plague. Home, she's relieved to be alive
in the age of the potato

with a Ryan Gosling chin. Tabs proliferate
like giant hogweed. She lies down in the green
blush of a Norwegian wildlife refuge
streaming on her laptop. Population:
three roe deer, a bean goose named Ruth.

She'll meet them in the apocalypse.
Bicycle, shipping container, seeds for trade.
Night slops into her condo like crude oil.
She waits for the sun to swipe her awake.

Twenty-first Century Adventure Novel

The male protagonist began
and ended his rock-climbing career
at Rattlesnake Point, trying to think
of something clever. He used to drink
a lot, was a shill for the Science Fiction
Square Dancing Society. He solved mysteries
with arcane knowledge from Russian
message boards, toured revolutionary countries
in a steampunk camper van—though
he picked up neither guitar nor saucepan.
He cloaked himself in high-performance
women, a soft shell

sponsorship. All those gorges
between his stories. They kept us hungry.

Ravens Bring News of the Future
After Wacousta *by John Richardson*

In general, the ravens reported,
owls were white pears. Webbed toes

were as sacred as the source of a crowing
river. Sons—little sons—hung

fish from thin pines, shoulders stern
with fever. The only city: vacant.

Ginger mist on the tide.
Torches, goslings, rashes

glowing at dusk.
The rest unspeakable

thirst.

Biometrics

In the waning days of the Internet,
the moon was a Donate Now link.
Tides stayed in for decades,
so women surrendered monthly

to the tug of livestreams:
rabbits multiplying on highway medians,
bald eagles padding nests with laptop
sleeves. Fingers were middle-class,

thumbs a luxury. Except through infrared,
infants went unseen for eighteen months.
Geese flew in HTML formation,
but migratory patterns remained encrypted.

The sky was a scarlet podcast.
Email a raccoon in hospital greens.

To Watch the Land Disappear
Into the Ocean
A cento

Texan vixens come sailing in,
rain falling into their open eyes.

Occasionally it's as cold as Ottawa,
ten thousand bees lighting on ice.

Whole winters without snow,
one eye on the horizon: a long, indeterminable

sun comes through the curtains like the plague.
People say drowning is the most peaceful way to die.

Winter of '15

You wouldn't remember porcupines,
but from the lake, the condos glinted

like quills. That was the winter we learned crows
could understand analogies. Decades later,

we'd breed them to speak. Those were the coldest months
in what was the world's hottest year. I walked three miles

to the juice bar to appease my Fitbit,
uphill both ways. We still dreamed

of Enceladus's hot springs, but back then, Saturn
felt as far away as April. That was the first season

a lab mouse woke with false memories.
You see, sleep often swaddled us

in fear. Here was a cure for what we knew
about the future. Forgive us.

It took so much
to raise a paw to those dark mornings.

Ferry Trip in Wildfire Season

A weary ghost sprawls across the Salish Sea
and we pass through its body—westbound
Queen of Cowichan, regal as a kidney stone.

The man bun in front of me lists
like a twenty-first century sundial, but smoke
is its own time zone, our bronchial tubes stuffed

with pine needles, daddy-long-legs,
mountain goat horns. While a shirtless boy
combs the cabin for his lost toy sword, I read

about penis worms. Allegedly,
we have burrowing dicks
to thank for the outbreak

of multicellular life. Or Earth's first
extinction event, depending.
Over the PA, the captain asks us to believe

in the Coast Mountains, even though we can't
see them. I picture glaciers
thawing like microwave dinners,

flash-frozen viruses surfacing like corn niblets.
My book has moved on to blastoids—Carboniferous
marine creatures whose fossils are often confused

for hickory nuts. I would've guessed Pokémon,
maybe cancer. An RCMP officer holsters
a newborn. A woman grips the pay-to-play

binoculars, diaper bag tick-tocking
against her hip. She yells "FIRE" but there's nowhere
to evacuate. The boy's recovered plastic

blade misses my kidney by a hare's
breath. Irritation, crisis. Split
by a tiny, anxious inhale.

Pastoral

At the beginning of the dust,
we will have chest X-rays,
lungs like blotched strawberries.

This is the landscape
toward the end of salad
spinners: supermarkets barren

as cathedrals, fish
evangelists preaching
from parched motel pools.

In the last years of birds,
the sky will fur up
like bread mold.

When the mountains shake
their manes, we'll say
the continent betrayed us.

What happened was this:
whitecaps, whitecaps
seven billion human beings.

Notes

"Actresses Fording the Dyea River on the Chilkoot Trail, 1867" shares its title with a photograph by Frank La Roche. The preferred name for the river is the Taiya.

"Frontier Diaries" is a suite of erasure poems that use as primary source material the memoirs and blogs of settler women in North America in the nineteenth, twentieth and twenty-first centuries. Each poem was carved from individual excerpts of the works cited below. While I maintained the order of words and letters in each excerpt, punctuation, formatting (i.e., italics) and poem titles are my own.

Drummond, Ree. *Confessions of a Pioneer Woman* (blog), *The Pioneer Woman*, accessed April–September, 2016.

Harrison, Erin. *Keeper of the Homestead* (blog), accessed July-September, 2016.

Langton, Anne. *A Gentlewoman in Upper Canada: The Journals of Anne Langton*, ed. H.H. Langton (Toronto, Vancouver: Clarke, Irwin & Company Limited, 1950).

Lister, Cheryl. *Off the Grid Mama* (blog), accessed July-September, 2016.

Moodie, Susanna. *Roughing It in the Bush, or Life in Canada*, ed. Carl Ballstadt (Ottawa: Carleton University Press, 1988).

Morritt, Hope. *Land of the Fireweed: A Young Woman's Story of Alaska Highway Construction Days* (Edmonds, Washington: Alaska Northwest Pub. Co., 1985).

Robins, Elizabeth. *The Alaska-Klondike Diary of Elizabeth Robin, 1900*, eds. Victoria Moessner and Joanne E. Gates (Fairbanks: University of Alaska Press, 1999).

"To Watch the Land Disappear into the Ocean" borrows its title and phrases from poems by Louise Glück, Aaron Belz, Carolyn Forché, Nelson Ball, Noelle Kocot, Mary Jo Bang, Margaret Atwood, John Ashbery, and Adam Sol.

The italicized lines in "Girls Gone Wild" describe plants using phrases from the following guides:

Government of Yukon. *Common Yukon roadside flowers* (Whitehorse: Government of Yukon Wildlife Viewing Program, 2019).

Derek Johnson, Linda Kershaw and Andy MacKinnon. *Plants of the Western Boreal Forest and*

Aspen Parkland (Edmonton: Lone Pine Publishing, 1995).

"Pastoral" quotes from the following sentence from Dana Goodyear's article "The Dying Sea" (*The New Yorker*, May 4, 2015):

"This is the landscape after people, you think. This is the landscape toward the end of the fish, in the last years of the birds, at the beginning of the dust."

Acknowledgments

Thank you to Leigh Nash, Julie Wilson, Megan Fildes, Andrew Faulkner, and everyone who makes books happen at Invisible. You are a dream team.

Thank you to Mum, Dad and Col for your constant love and support.

I could not have finished this book without the encouragement and critical eye of fellow poet and co-conspirator, Katie Jordon.

Thanks to Ariel Gordon for the poem exchanges, the sparkling conversations, and the loveliest blurb a girl could ask for.

And to John Irving: I will always be grateful for your deep consideration of my work.

To the EG—your brilliant words show me what it means to be a poet. See you in April.

Earlier versions of some poems in this collection appeared in the following publications: *CV2*, *Room*, *The Puritan*, and *Hamilton Arts & Letters*. Thank you to the editors for taking such care with my work. Thanks, also, to Yvonne Blomer for selecting "Sounds a River

Makes" for the anthology *Sweet Water: Poems for the Watersheds* (Caitlin Press, 2020).

I am deeply grateful to the Writers Trust of Canada and the Klondike Visitors' Association for the three glorious, life-changing months I spent at the Berton House in Dawson City. To Nick, Gen, Meg, Chuck, Eryn, Kathy, both Dan D.s, Norma, Dan S., Laurie, Emile, Abbi, Joey, Joan, Don, Bob, Sally, and everyone I crossed paths with in the Yukon: thank you for your hospitality, your warmth, and your stories.

I wrote and lived these poems on the traditional territories of the Huron-Wendat, the Anishnaabeg, the Mississaugas of the Credit, the Haudenosaunee, the Omàmiwinini (Algonquin), and the Tr'ondëk Hwëch'in. This was and continues to be an immense privilege made possible by the stewardship and generosity of these Indigenous communities. I am the beneficiary of this country's ongoing history of colonialism; my awareness of this, and of my own complicity, has informed these poems.

INVISIBLE PUBLISHING produces fine Canadian literature for those who enjoy such things. As an independent, not-for-profit publisher, our work includes building communities that sustain and encourage engaging, literary, and current writing.

Invisible Publishing has been in operation for over a decade. We released our first fiction titles in the spring of 2007, and our catalogue has come to include works of graphic fiction and non-fiction, pop culture biographies, experimental poetry, and prose.

We are committed to publishing diverse voices and experiences. In acknowledging historical and systemic barriers, and the limits of our existing catalogue, we strongly encourage LGBTQ2SIA+, Indigenous, and writers of colour to submit their work.

Invisible Publishing is also home to the Bibliophonic series of music books and the Throwback series of CanLit reissues.

If you'd like to know more please get in touch:
info@invisiblepublishing.com

Invisible